How To Be A

The Definitive Guide

By Rab McRadge

Any spelling, grammar or punctuation errors in this book are entirely due to the fact that I am a Bawbag and proud of it.

ISBN: 9781977096692

Contents

Introduction

Bawbags are on the rise. From their humble beginnings in Scotland, they are beginning to spread their numbers and influence all over the world. This influence is visible in music, tv and film. It has most recently began to influence the world of global politics, the evidence of this seen prominently in The White House itself.

But am I a Bawbag?

This is a question many people ask themselves as they look into the mirror, because being a Bawbag is more desirable than it has ever been before. Women may spend money on make-up, perfume, clothes and plastic surgery in an attempt to reach the pinnacle of womanhood. Well the pinnacle of manhood is to be a Bawbag.

This book is the definitive guide to becoming a true Bawbag. Written by the natural born Bawbag Rab McRadge, it is the only text you will ever need in order to reach your lofty goal.

Chapter 1: History Of The Bawbag

In the context of the origins of the homo-bawbagus, the BawbAlba expansion refers to the cultural dispersal of the Bawbags from the country of Scotland to the rest of the world. There are two separate theories of how this dispersal occurred. These are the Weegie-Bawbagus Dispersal and the Kirkcaldy-Bawbagus Dispersal. Both are discussed in this chapter.

Origins

Weegie-Bawbagus

Some Bawbagologists believe that the first Bawbags originated in the city of Glasgow on the West coast of Scotland. The mixture of Irish Catholics, Protestants and Highland haggis shaggers was an interesting one as the city grew in industrial times. Some believe that there was the mix of inbreeding and cross-breeding of Irish Catholics, Protestants, Highlanders and rats created the modern Bawbag. Any visitor to Glasgow today will marvel at the number of pure Bawbags inhabiting the city. Religious divides there maybe, but everyone knows that all Celtic and Rangers fans are fucking Bawbags!

<u>Kirkcaldy-Bawbagus</u>

This other branch of Bawbagology believe that all Bawbags originated in the town of Kircaldy on the East coast of Scotland. Not many tourists visit Kirkcaldy, but if they do they will encounter a whole town of Bawbags.

From piss head dart World Champion Jocky Wilson, to piss-pot Prime Minister Gordon Brown, there have been a few famous Kirkcaldy Bawbags to hit the world stage. Adam Smith, who many call the father of economics and the father of capitalism, was a Kirkcaldy born Bawbag. All the poor fuckers today standing in assembly lines all the fucking time, doing menial tasks as they waste their life away in boredom, can blame fucking Bawbag Adam Smith for inventing that shit. This mind numbing work dulls the brain of a man, and believers in the Kirkcaldy-Bawbagus dispersal believe that a dull brain is the main cause of Bawbag syndrome. Therefore, Kirkcaldy Bawbag Adam Smith may be the father of economics and capitalism, but his true gift to the world is as the father of Bawbagism.

Anybody who visits Kirkcaldy will quickly become a believer in this theory of Bawbag dispersal.

How The Bawbags Spread Globally

How these Bawbags spread from their local area across the world, eventually finding themselves proudly sitting in The White House itself, is a source of great debate. Again, the Weegie-Bawbagus followers and the Kirkcaldy-Bawbagusies are divided. Kirkcaldy-Bawbagusies believe it was spread through the work of Adam Smith as mentioned before, but the Weegie-Bawbagusies have a very different idea:

It was all the work of the lethal combination of Big Rab C Nesb and Buckfast.

The following chapters of this book explain how to be an effective Bawbag. But whether you believe in the Weegie or the Kirkcaldy Bawbag theory, following the example of Rab C. Nesb and drinking bucket loads of Buckfast is a good way to achieve Bawbagdom.

Chapter 2: A Bawbag At The Bar

Bawbags belong in bars. It is their natural habitat. Originally, Bawbags could only be found in the dives of Scotland, but due to the expanding Bawbag population and development, they can now be found in many bars around the planet.

Bawbags drink cheap alcohol. A Bawbag never drinks wine. A Bawbag never drinks effeminate drinks. A Bawbag drinks cheap gassy lager, cheap whisky, cheap vodka or cheap cider (made without apples). Super-strength lager is desirable if served in the bar. If not, a true Bawbag will sneak said drink into the bar in his coat pockets. A Bawbag may also have a hipflask in the pub. A Bawbag's aim is to get blind drunk as cheaply as possible.

In fact, a clever Bawbag will try to pay as little as possible, getting many drinks for free from his mates. When out with a group of mates on a pub crawl, a Bawbag will ensure that he buys the round in the cheapest pub. Or he may just buy the first round in the first pub. Then hope that by the time it gets back to his round again, his mates will be too drunk to remember whose round it is. He will then stay quiet until somebody else gets the round in. This often effectively works until the end of the evening. As all Bawbags know, the drunker people get the more likely they are to buys rounds for their mates. A good Bawbag will take advantage of this. An expert Bawbag will only buy between 0 and 1 round in any night out.

In busy bars and clubs, a Bawbag has a range of tactics to prevent himself from spending too much time ordering drinks. A Bawbag looks for people he knows in these kind of places. Gullible and drunk people. He will invest in a round of drinks on this occasion to avoid ordering at the bar. The Bawbag will approach this gullible drunk acquaintance and chat to them for a short time. The Bawbag will then mention that he needs a piss and give the gullible drunk some money to get a round in. Preferably this will not be enough money for the full round. The Bawbag will then leave the gullible drunk to get the round in, while he himself goes to chat to other mates or to try to get a suitable woman. Thus, Bawbag does not need to wait at the bar. After a period of time, the Bawbag will return to find the gullible drunk back from the bar with the drinks. The Bawbag will then chat to the gullible drunk while drinking his drink. Bawbag will then tell the gullible drunk that it is his round, and he is then free to leave for some fun again as the gullible drunk returns to the bar once more. This is a tactic of a high level Bawbag.

If a Bawbag does have to go to a busy bar, he often orders Guinness. He be served by one member of the bar staff, who will complete the 1st pour of the pint, then leave it to settle. In busy bars, this bar staff person will go to serve another customer while the pint settles. The Bawbag will alert the attention of another member of the bar staff and ask them to top up the pint. He will then take the pint and walk away saying he has already paid for it. This only works in very busy bars, with a large number of bar staff. It also only works if you are a true expert Bawbag.

If ordering a full round however, this tactic can't be used. Even a Bawbag has to negotiate the difficult process of getting served at a busy bar. In the UK, lines of people cram at the bar each desperately trying to get the attention of the bar staff in order to get served next. Otherwise, a man can spend far too much time waiting at the bar. This is wasted drinking time and may prevent a Bawbag from attaining a woman that evening. Therefore, Bawbags have developed specific skills for getting served quickly in these situations.

When a Bawbag reaches the bar, he first puts both of his elbow onto the bar itself. He then spread his legs as wide as is possible to either side of him. He then repeats this process with his elbows. When a customer next to him leaves the bar, a Bawbag spreads his legs and elbows wider still, preventing a new customer reaching the bar. A Bawbag will lean his head as far over the bar as possible and repeatedly call to the bar staff until he is served. If a group of Bawbags are together getting a round in, they can all execute the legs/elbow spread technique and can effectively conquer a large area of the bar.

A Bawbag's sharp senses and attention skills mean that he will always spot when somebody has left their drink unattended in busy bars. Now with the spiking of drinks, this is more dangerous than previously for Bawbags, but it is still worth the risk for a free drink. The most common drink abandoners are females who leave their drinks to hit the dance floor. Because females drink spirits, it makes it easier for the scavenger Bawbag to swoop in and quickly down the unattended drinks unnoticed. Even if the Bawbag is caught, he is used to the level pf abuse that will be directed at him. He will calmly point out that there was nobody there so he thought they were left overs. Then he will walk away. Mission complete. But most of the time, an expert Bawbag will never get caught.

Bawbag At The Bar Checklist:

Skill/Strategy	Achieved
Drink Cheap Shit	
Sneak Drinks In	
Avoid Rounds	
Gullible Drunk Technique	
Guinness Steal	
Legs/Elbows Spread	
Scavenger Bawbag	

A Bawbag says,

always piss in the pool

Chapter 3: Dance Like A Bawbag

A Bawbag owns the dancefloor. All eyes are drawn to the Bawbag as he bounds around all over the place, bumping into others and ensuring that he is the dominant male there. A Bawbag is never a good dancer. This is not the Bawbag way. In fact, a true Bawbag will bump into any good dancers on the dancefloor, ensuring that they realise that being a good dancer is not essential to being successful on the dancefloor. Being a Bawbag is.

A Bawbag uses every inch of the dancefloor and anyone who gets in his way, must expect a bashing. This ensures that people make space for the Bawbag and a Bawbag needs lots of space for his particular dancing manoeuvres.

The Bawbag dancing style began in the mid-1980s with the arrival of the British ska music scene. Raising their knees high into the air and rarely moving their arms, they looked like drunken chickens. However, it has since developed so that all limbs of the Bawbags are moving aggressively wildly.

Bawbag dancing can develop strong bodies, but it is important that the Bawbag lacks spatial awareness. While some dancing styles require dedication and serious training, Bawbag dancing requires incompetence and serious drinking. Unlike other dancing styles, Bawbag dancing is not possible to execute sober, making it unique in the world of dance.

Here are some steps to help you to begin to master the art of Bawbag dancing.

Getting Ready To Dance

Inebriate your body thoroughly. Drinking alcohol is important to loosen your inhibitions. It is vital that it is done before a performance of Bawbag dancing. It is essential to drink for at least 3 to 4 hours prior to a performance to give the body ample time to warm up, and to reduce the risk of thinking about what you are doing. Remember, thinking inhibits the ability to be a Bawbag on the dancefloor.

Entering The Dancefloor

Make an instant impression when you enter the dancefloor. Everybody must know you have arrives. By everybody, I don't just mean everybody on the dancefloor but everybody in the building. To ensure your success in this area, shout a war cry as you step onto the dancefloor and then strike an initial pose. This is akin to the entrance of a wrestler, you must make an instant impression. After this, and this is important, look into the eyes of somebody staring at you and tell them to 'Fuck off!'. This sets the tone for your dancing performance. A clever Bawbag will chose a tame person for this, therefore avoiding a fight.

Facial Expressions

No part of your face should remain still at any time of the performance. The mouth must constantly move, smiling, grinning, opening as you shout and laugh, lips quivering, teeth chattering. The eyes must remain intense throughout, looking at the others who watch you, daring them to challenge you. Scrunch your nose up repeatedly and flex your eyebrows as much as you can at all times. Puff out your cheeks, wink and screw up your eyes. Your face must be a performance in itself.

Body Movements

There must be no rules, no order to the movements of the Bawbag's body. Arms and legs must never rest, but the movement must be uncoordinated, exaggerated and poorly timed. Point at innocent bystanders both on and at the side of the dancefloor, preferably those most disgusted by your performance. Remember to bump into others and maybe even elbow or kick them in your movements. Just ensure you do not do this to hard guys who may attack. But a Bawbag may sneakily bump into a goof, hence knocking them into a hard man. The Bawbag will then enjoy watching the goof get his ass kicked.

Shouting And Singing

A Bawbag will shout obscenities and sing during the performance. When singing, sing loudly so everyone can hear you and sing out of tune. Get the words to the song wrong, inserting swear words that should not be there. Or sing a completely different song, maybe a football song or a wrestler's entrance song. And don't forget to randomly shout those obscenities like, "Come the fuck on!" and "Here we fucking go now!"

Master these techniques effectively and you will be an expert Bawbag dancer.

Dancing Like A Bawbag Checklist:

Skill/Strategy	Achieved
Getting Ready To Dance	
Entering The Dancefloor	
Bump Into Others	
Own The Whole Floor	
Facial Expressions	
Body Movements	
Shouting + Singing	

A Bawbag says,

shit happens

no problem

it will decompose

Chapter 4: Dine Like A Bawbag

The etiquette involved in dining is complicated for most people to master. What makes it more complicated is that different cultures around the world follow different rules. Luckily, the etiquette involved in dining like a Bawbag transcends all cultures. Wherever a Bawbag goes, he is still a Bawbag. Unlike other people who try to fit in, a Bawbag never fits in. That is his culture. To always stand out as a Bawbag. So Bawbag dining etiquette is the same all over the world. Here are its rules:

Napkin Etiquette

1. At the beginning of the meal take the napkin, blow your nose with it then place it on the table next to your food.

2. At some point during the meal, wipe your face with the napkin and blow your nose with the napkin repeatedly.

3. At the end of the meal, throw the napkin into the face of the person you would most describe as a wanker at the table.

Handling Utensils

1. Hold the knife, fork and spoon in any fucking way you want to.

When To Start Eating

1. In informal settings, eat as soon as the food arrives.

2. On formal occasions, eat as soon as the food arrives.

Resting Utensils

1. If you need to leave your knife and fork when taking a break and are not finished eating, stab them into some food so that they make a 'v' sign in the direction of the person at the table you would most describe as a wanker.

2. If however you are finished with your food, steal them.

Announcing That You Need To Leave The Table

A Bawbag is blunt. Loudly and proudly say, "I need a piss" or "I need a dump". Then just get up and go.

Commenting On The Food

1. If the food was good, burp and fart loudly.

2. If the food was shit, tell everyone this then chuck it at the wanker.

Dine Like A Bawbag Checklist:

Skill/Strategy	Achieved
Napkin Etiquette	
Handling Utensils	
When To Start	
Resting Utensils	
Leaving The Table	
Commenting	

A Bawbag says,

farting is

sharing

and sharing is

caring

Chapter 5:

Being A Bawbag On The Train

1. When getting onto the train, a Bawbag does not wait for others to get off. Other non-Bawbags will do this so this give the Bawbag the opportunity to get on first and get the best (or only) seat. Push past anybody who gets in your way and make sure you get the seat you want.

2. Make sure that you receive a phone call while you are on the train and if you don't, just pretend that you do. Then talk as loudly as you possibly can about rude things using obscenities. This will ensure that you annoy as many people as possible. Etiquette expert Nicholas Smythe says that, "People who receive phone calls on public transport should always be mindful of other passengers. Speak quietly and finish the call quickly, arranging a suitable time to receive the call when you are no longer on public transport." A Bawbag says, "Fuck Nicholas Smythe and his bull shetiquette!"

3. Women often annoy other by putting on make-up on the train. If a Bawbag sees a woman do this, he will of course inform her that she is still ugly. But a Bawbag has his own similar personal grooming tactic to piss off other passenger. A Bawbag's chosen method is nose picking. A Bawbag will happily pick his nose, putting his finger deep into the nostril in order to collect all the bogies within. A Bawbag will then either eat this bogie, wipe it on the seat

in front, or flick it at the passenger they believe to be the best example of a wanker present.

4. A Bawbag will never give up his seat for an old person, pregnant women or anyone. If somebody like this is in need to a seat, a Bawbag pretends to fall asleep.

5. A Bawbag will eat the smelliest, loudest food possible throughout the journey. Crisps, hot food, smelly cheese, anything that is basically smelly or noisy. And he will do this whilst drinking alcohol, burping and farting. Throughout the journey.

6. A Bawbag on a train will at some point remove his shoes and socks and cut his toenails. He will dispense of these toenails by flicking them in various directions in the direction of as many different passengers as possible.

7. A Bawbag plays music as loudly as he can and sings along out of tune. Never play popular songs, but those most likely to offend.

Bawbag On A Train Checklist:

Skill/Strategy	Achieved
Getting On The Train	
Phone Calls	
Personal Grooming	
Giving Up Your Seat	
Eating	
Toenail Clipping	
Music	

A Bawbag says,

Love is

still holding in your farts

after you get married

Chapter 6:
Bawbag Drinking Games + Activities

Bawbag Cocktails

Two Bawbags go up to a bar. The first Bawbag must order a cocktail consisting of three random words. It must not be a real cocktail. For example, "Wild Monkey Piss". The bar staff will be confused so the second Bawbag must quickly invent this drink by taking the first letter of each of these three words and choosing three drinks that begin with each of these letters. Only one of these three drinks is allowed to be non-alcoholic. For example, "**W**ild **M**onkey **P**iss" = **W**hisky, **M**idori and **P**ernod. Bawbag two must then down this drink. One Bawbag can also play this game with a non-Bawbag, getting the non-Bawbag absolutely wasted in the process. A clever Bawbag will practice for this game, learning the weakest and best drinks to go with each letter of the alphabet. The non-Bawbag will be destroyed.

The Turn Me Down Contest

When a Bawbag is out for a night with some shy non-Bawbag mates and said Bawbag, the Turn Me Down Contest is a good way of making his boring mates more interesting and productive. The Bawbag will suggest this game to his unwitting mates, in what is a piece of reverse psychology genius. The aim for each player is to get turned down by as many woman as possible. All inhibitions go out the window as failure becomes success. You can try incredibly bad chat-up lines, try to get with women way out of your league and watch your mates do the same, all in the knowledge that you score a point every time a woman tells you she is not interested. At the end of this contest, it is amazing how many of your gang actually get a woman. The one who actually wins the contest, is a fucking wanker of the highest order.

Toasting The Birds

Sit at a table where many women are going to walk past. Every time a really fit woman walks past the table, down your drink. Every time an ugly woman walks past, take a drink. Every time a minger walks past, clinked your class in a cheers salute with your mates and take a drink. Remember, this game is about personal taste. A Bawbag develops really high standards as this game goes on, never seeing a really fit girl while his mates continue to down drinks, getting absolutely fucked. If one of his mate's girlfriends walks past, a Bawbag looks at his mate and says, "Cheers".

A Bawbag says,

one man's minger

is another

man's wife

Chapter 7: Romance Like A Bawbag

It's amazing given their uncouth habits and general disregard for others, that Bawbag's have any success at pulling. But a Bawbag know the desperate hour, when the night is nearly over and the last chance to pull comes. He can spot the women on the rebound or those whose senses are befuddled. This is the Bawbag's only chance of success.

However, let's celebrate the many failures of the Bawbag when attempting to pull. These are far more common than their successes and these failures are the true measure of a Bawbag.

A Bawbag has not got any idea what to say to a woman. His mundane chat-up techniques include asking them if they watched the game, or telling them about his mate Dave, or explaining exactly what he has had to drink that night. At times he tries more original chat-up lines, when he is trying to be romantic or seductive. Here are a selection of the worst examples of this:

- I like my women like I like my beer… to go down easy.

- You know I can't dance and I don't romance, but if you give me the chance, I'll electrify your pants.

- I'm better than Santa Claus cos I've got two sacks full of presents for you.

None of these have ever worked. A Bawbag is never romantic or seductive, but always believes that he is.

A Bawbag will always do his best to ensure that none of his mates pull. When a friend is trying to impress a girl, a Bawbag will bring up inappropriate things like all the mingers his mate has shagged or he will ask the girl questions about her ex-boyfriends and sex life. If the girl has a mate, the Bawbag will attempt to chat her up maybe using his chat-up lines. The girl his friend is attempting to get with will then have to go to her friend's rescue thus ending his friend's chance of success.

Bawbag On The Pull Checklist:

Skill/Strategy	Achieved
Mundane Chat-Up Lines	
Original Chat-Up Lines	
Ruin A Mate's Chances	

A Bawbag says,

getting married is like

drinking Tennent's Super

the headache is

just around the corner

Chapter 8:

Being A Bawbag Of A Husband

Let me start this chapter with a tale of a married Bawbag at Christmas:

The Married Bawbag At Christmas

The married Bawbag woke up on Christmas morning and went for a walk. He knocked on his neighbour's door. His neighbour Jon opened the door. He was surprised to see the married Bawbag in his dressing gown. "Merry Christmas Bawbag," said Jon.

"Bah humbug!" the married Bawbag shouted at Jon then smacked him in the face. The married Bawbag walked away laughing.

Then the married Bawbag went to the local shop. He picked up some milk and eggs. Strangely he then opened the eggs and started throwing them at people in the shop. Everyone ran out the shop.

"Ho Ho Ho! Merry Christmas!" the married Bawbag shouted at them.

After this, the married Bawbag went to the town square. He saw the town Christmas tree and he charged it.

When he got to the Christmas tree, he rugby tackled it to the floor. An old lady shouted at him so he threw eggs at her and wished her a, "Merry Christmas." The old woman ran away.

Finally the married Bawbag got home. His wife was just getting out of bed. "Merry Christmas Bawbag. Where have you been?" she asked him.

"I went to get milk," he said. The married Bawbag then opened the milk and poured it on his wife's head. "Merry Christmas wife," he said. Then he put his clothes on, went out and poured the rest of the milk on his own head. And that's why he is a Bawbag.

I'm sure you are not surprised that very few Bawbags actually get married, but those that do are the worst husbands ever. In fact, it is said some men only true become a Bawbag after they get married. They begin to relax after years of striving to reach perfection in order to attract a mate. Once they are married and finally relax, their true inner Bawbag come out and their true calling in life is unleashed. Here are some things that a married Bawbag must do to ensure he is the dominant force in the marriage:

1. After marriage, be the first to fart in bed.

2. Your 1st attempt at cooking must be awful, so you are never asked to do it again.

3. Control the tv. Sport must be on at all times. If there are no matches on, the sports news should be on. If your wife is the type to attempt to watch soaps, get another tv or preferably another wife.

4. If your wife shouts at you, ignore her. Watch the telly or read a paper while she shouts. You can win this argument without words.

5. If your wife is upset, tell her to text her mate.

6. If your wife wants your opinion on something, tell her to text her mate.

7. If your wife makes a 'I don't know why you..." comment. For example, "I don't know why you don't make the bed." Or, "I don't know why you never do the dishes." Or, "I don't know why you insist on getting hammered, spewing on the carpet and pissing on the dog." Always answer, "Google it."

8. Never trust your wife.

9. If your wife makes you go shopping with her, embarrass the fuck out of her. Dress like a tramp so she feels shamed in front of the people she knows who you bump into. Carry a hipflask in your pocket and make sure that you take a swig from it when your wife is talking to somebody she knows. If your wife does talk to somebody she knows ask your wife embarrassing questions like, "Do

we need any shite paper?" or "Is this your mate that you said had a fat arse?"

10. When your wife returns home from somewhere, always greet her with a fart or a burp.

11. Regularly leave your wife gifts. Hide dirty socks under the bed, sweaty t-shirts under the sofa and dirty pants under her pillow.

12. It is essential to forget your anniversary, your wife's birthday and Valentine's Day. This will save a Bawbag a lot of money.

13. Do not do what you say you'll do. If you tell her that you are going to do the dishes, leave the fuckers in the sink until she does them. When she reminds you that you said you'd do them, tell her you forgot.

14. When your wife is speaking to you, master the art of pretending to listen.

15. When arranging to meet, always be late. Really late. Assume she will be late. She is a woman after all. To ensure you are the last to arrive, find a place near the meeting venue where you can see if your wife has arrived yet. Always make sure you arrive at least 10 minutes after her. Then, you win.

16. Learn how to lie convincingly.

17. Maximize laziness. True laziness is not doing something you know you should do. Lie in bed until late afternoon and master the art of remaining in your armchair for as long as possible. If she wants something, stay there until she gets it herself. Then, you win.

18. If you have a baby, never change the nappies.

19. If you have a baby and you fart, the wife will assume that the baby has done a poo. Watch your wife attempt to change the baby's nappy knowing that there is no poo. She will waste her time and she will assume that the baby has farted. Bawbag baby!

20. If you have a boy, bring up that boy to be a Bawbag.

21. If you have a girl, the wife can deal with her.

There is no check list for being a Bawbag of a husband because the list of things you need to do is endless. Being a married Bawbag is very hard work. To achieve a successful Bawbaged marriage takes years of hard work, flexibility and determination. It is said by many, that this is a Bawbag's greatest achievement of all.

A Bawbag says,

the world is your toilet,

wherever you go

make yourself at home,

leave your own special scent,

and leave others to sort out
your shit

Chapter 9: A Bawbag Abroad

Travelling to a new country and experiencing a different culture can be one of the most wondrous ways of opening one's eyes and broadening one's horizons. A Bawbag doesn't give a fuck about any of that shite, he just wants to get pished in a different place.

Middle-class British travellers are often quiet and reserved when abroad, not wanting to draw unwanted attention to themselves. A Bawbag demands attention. He will shout at all times, wear stereotypical clothes of that country or his own, and throw litter on the street. He will loudly comment on and/or complain about things native to the country he is visiting, making sure that he is heard by the locals and trying to insult as many of them as possible. Here are some examples of what he may say:

"THESE SPANISH ARE LAZY BASTARDS WITH THEIR FUCKING SIESTAS!" A Bawbag loves to wake up the locals during siesta nap time.

Please remember, I am not insulting any nationality in this chapter. Although some Spanish people are poor excuses for men, many are actually Bawbags and they are a great source of pride for that nation.

In fact, there are Bawbags and non-Bawbags in every country and religion in the world. The Bawbag sect is inclusive of all colours, creeds, religions and nationalities. It is also not homophobic. There are many gay Bawbags. The Bawbag sect is only sexist. Well and actually hair-style-ist, nose-ist, ear-ist, footballteam-ist, car-ist, house-ist, well actually everything-ist. Bawbags respect all other Bawbags. Everyone else can go shag a goat!

Back To The Quotes:

"You need that sombrero to make sure those bloody ears don't get burnt mate. Where I come from, you'd be called bugger lugs."

"Fondue is it called? Fucking melted cheese strings mate."

"Sushi's what? Raw fish? Cheap bastards don't even cook it! Fucking rip off!"

Actually, the Americans tend to be natural Bawbags abroad.

A Bawbag abroad is always drunk. He travels around the world to never see any historical buildings or landmarks. A Bawbag would describe Notre Dame in Paris as 'A big fuckin church' and the Eiffel Tower as "a big tower full of wankers". These cultural delights do not interest a Bawbag. He can see them any time he wants back home on Google. A Bawbag abroad's sole aim is to get rat-arsed and try to get a local woman. He will never, ever get a local woman by the way.

Locals will shake their head at the Bawbag, angry that they are polluting their country. Hence, Bawbags abroad often get into fights and get arrested. A Bawbag will always loudly exclaim the country he is from so that the locals know who he represents. The wrong country. His own country's national enemies.

For example, if a Scottish Bawbag cause bother in a Turkish bar, he will proudly sing English songs. He will then have further hurt the English reputation abroad. Clever Bawbag.

In many countries some subject are taboo and should never be discussed in public. While most travellers research local customs, history, food and places to visit before travelling to a foreign country, a Bawbag is different. A Bawbag will research these taboo topics before travelling abroad instead and bring them up in discussion with every local he meets. He will ensure that he takes the side of the argument most opposed to the general view of that country.

Bawbag Abroad Checklist:

Skill/Strategy	Achieved
Insult Local Customs	
Get Hammered	
Fail To Attract Local Women	
Pretend To Be From Rival Country	
Discuss Taboo Subjects With Locals	

A Bawbag says,

freedom is

pissing in public

Chapter 10: Are You A Bawbag?

So you have read the book and tried to put the advice from it into practice. Now it is time to see if you are truly a Bawbag. Complete this checklist yourself, and then ask a friend and a female you know to do so too. If you have 20 ticks or more from these 3 completed check lists, you are a Bawbag.

The Ultimate Bawbag Checklist:

For You To Complete:

Skill/Strategy	Achieved
Are You A Bawbag At The Bar?	
Do You Dance Like A Bawbag?	
Do You Dine Like A Bawbag?	
Do You Travel Like A Bawbag?	
Do You Look Like A Bawbag?	
Completed Bawbag Drinking Games?	
Romance Like A Bawbag?	
Are You a Bawbag Husband?	
Are You A Bawbag Abroad?	

For Your Mate To Complete:

Skill/Strategy	Achieved
Are You A Bawbag At The Bar?	
Do You Dance Like A Bawbag?	
Do You Dine Like A Bawbag?	
Do You Travel Like A Bawbag?	
Do You Look Like A Bawbag?	
Completed Bawbag Drinking Games?	
Romance Like A Bawbag?	
Are You a Bawbag Husband?	
Are You A Bawbag Abroad?	

For A Female To Complete:

Skill/Strategy	Achieved
Are You A Bawbag At The Bar?	
Do You Dance Like A Bawbag?	
Do You Dine Like A Bawbag?	
Do You Travel Like A Bawbag?	
Do You Look Like A Bawbag?	
Completed Bawbag Drinking Games?	
Romance Like A Bawbag?	
Are You a Bawbag Husband?	
Are You A Bawbag Abroad?	

Number Of Ticks:	
Are You A Bawbag?	

Thank you for reading this book. If you have completed the challenge, you are now officially a Bawbag. If you have not, read it all again and resit the test.

Even if you are now a Bawbag, keep this book for reference. You must work hard to be a Bawbag. Not everyone can achieve this level of Bawbagity.

And remember,

wherever you go,

A Bawbag is a Bawbag

Rab McRadge: Master Bawbag

Printed in Great Britain
by Amazon

34292086R00026